AG

SANTERÍA AND THE ORISHA OF VOLCANOES AND THE WILDERNESS

by Baba Raul Canizares

ORIGINAL PUBLICATIONS
PLAINVIEW, NEW YORK

AGANJÚ
SANTERÍA AND THE ORISHA OF VOLCANOES AND THE WILDERNESS

© ORIGINAL PUBLICATIONS 2003

ISBN: 0-942272-70-6

FIRST EDITION
First Printing 2003

Original Publications
P.O. Box 236
Old Bethpage, New York 11804-0236
1-888-OCCULT-1

Printed in the United States of America

INTRODUCTION

It was a cold Spring night in that magical part of Manhattan called the East Village. I was visiting Lady Armida's Witchcraft Shop on 6th street. Armida, a Wiccan high priestess who gave classes out of her store and led a large coven, at that time in association with famed Witch activist and author Dr. Leo Martello, had received some primary Santería initiations from me after I had performed a series of lectures for her students. In fact, her entire coven ended up receiving Orisha necklaces and/or Warriors from me, this led to Armida becoming a close associate of mine. On that particular Spring night, Armida wanted me to perform a reading for a young Japanese woman who suspected her young Moroccan husband was cheating on her. She also wanted to "tie down" her man so he wouldn't be able to stray from her again. She offered to pay me three thousand dollars to perform this service for her. I told the young woman that, in principle, I was opposed to tying anyone down, as I strongly believed in respecting each person's right to make choices. To be honest, the three thousand dollars did sound tempting, so I agreed to perform a reading where, if it came out that the two of them were meant for each other, I would do as she requested. The Japanese lady managed to convince her husband to come meet me.

The young man did not look as I imagined a Moroccan should look yes, even I can fall victim to stereotyping—He was tall and white, with aquiline features and a continental air about him. I began to read the Spanish cards for him, when I suddenly felt my consciousness ebbing away, and I realized that my body was being taken over by a powerful spirit. I had been a spirit medium since the age of seven, so the sensation I was experiencing was not alien to me. What's unusual about this story is that I had not tried to call any spirit at that time, in fact, this was to be the first time since I had developed my faculties as a medium that a spirit took me over against my will, or by surprise. The spirit that took me over was Saborissa, an aspect of the Orisha Aganjú.

There were eight people present at that time, including Armida, the Japanese woman, and the young Moroccan. Saborissa manifested as a larger-than-life force. My already imposing 6'4" frame seemed to double as Saborissa stood up and with a thunderous voice demanded some rum. It happened that Armida had a gallon of Bacardi 151 on hand. Much to the astonishment of those present, Saborissa chug-a-lugged the rum as if it were water, then asked for more. Someone rushed out to a liquor store to get another bottle. In the meantime, Saborissa said that the young man, a Moroccan Muslim who had never heard of Santería, was a son of Aganjú and that he was to be a priest of the Orisha of volcanoes. He also told the startled young Arab that from that moment on he was to study the way of the Orisha under Baba Raul Canizares, whose body Saborissa was borrowing at that moment.

Saborissa then told the astounded young woman that she was not allowed to "tie" her husband down, and furthermore, Aganjú did not think she was good for him. When I came back into my body, I witnessed a weird scene where a handsome young man was crying, prostrated in front of me, his wife standing next to him looking extremely upset, shouting what I must assume were Japanese obscenities at me, and an extremely worried Lady Armida hoping I was okay, after she saw my body ingest a gallon of 151 proof alcohol, a lethal dose under normal circumstances. This whole surreal scene happened six years ago. Today, Adel Gabara, as the young Arab man is called, is still serving Aganjú and still learning from me. He and his Japanese wife were divorced long ago, and all because of an apparently chance encounter with the enormously life-changing power of a Force called Aganjú.

Aganjú—also spelled Agayu, Agallu, and Argayu in Cuba—is the personified spirit of the volcano and of the open spaces of wilderness in the Lukumi/Santería tradition which took shape in Cuba but originated among the Yoruba people of Southwestern Nigeria, in Africa. One cannot understand Santería unless one looks at Santería's antecedents.

Santería is neither a re-created religion, such as Wicca, nor a new religion. Its roots go back uninterruptedly at least as far as any other of the living, ancient, faiths. The religion we now refer to as "Santería" began, like all life, in Africa. Specifically, it began in the Nile valley, among a people called the "Twa" (also spelled "Kwa"). From the original Twa grouping, four major branches developed and traveled away from the center; those to the north became known as Ta-Merrians or Aegyptians, those to the South as Amazulus, those to the east as Agikuyus, and those to the west as Yoruba.' Forty thousand years ago, the Twa conceived of God in a way that became the basis of many African religions. The Twa called their God simply Greatest Creator of All—The Unknown. The Ta-Merrians called this God Aten, While the Yoruba called him Olodumare.

Yoruba civilization goes back at least a thousand years to the founding of Ile-Ife, holy city of the Yoruba and center of their empire. Yoruba scholars have advanced diverse ideas as to the origin of the Yoruba people, some even suggesting a relationship to Middle Eastern countries. The staff of Oranyan, a millenarian monolith, symbol of the Yoruba, has what appears to be the Hebrew letter "yod" carved near its pinnacle.

When European merchants, dealers in human suffering, arrived at the shores of West Africa in the sixteenth century, the magnificence of Yoruba culture had already begun to wane. However, exquisite works of art, especially in sculpture, attest to the greatness of the civilization that spread from Ife to a great part of Western Africa. The Yoruba achieved legendary status not only in art but also in religion. The beauty of Yoruba religious stories rival those of Ancient Greece.

The disintegration of the Yoruba empire can be traced to the fall of Alafin Awole in 1796, who is said to have cursed his people right before taking his own life. Muslim invasions by Fulani tribesmen in the early part of the nineteenth century resulted in hundreds of thousands of Yoruba finding themselves in chains, many losing their lives and being shipped to the New World as slaves in the infamous Middle Passage.

Among the Yoruba, Olodumare—also called Olorun—was the greatest of all divinities, the one who parceled out portions of Ashe, the source of all power, among the lesser divinities, called Orisha. The High God Olodumare was thought to be too far removed from humankind to help with everyday problems; for this the Yoruba and their New World descendants turned to the Orisha.

The main area of Yorubaland lies in the southwestern part of Nigeria, though considerable numbers of Yoruba live in the neighboring countries of Benin and Ghana. During the dark and shameful days of the slave trade, hundreds of thousands of the Yoruba were taken from their homeland and sold as chattels in North, Central, and South America, as well as in the Caribbean. In certain parts of the New World, particularly in places where the dominant religion was Catholicism, the Yoruba were able to preserve important elements of their faith. They were particularly successful in preserving their culture in Cuba, where they became known as Lucumi, and in Brazil, where they became known as Nago. The term Yoruba originally referred only to the people of the city-state of Oyo; it first was used to refer to all other members of the Ife hegemony in the nineteenth century, the term first being applied to the common language spoken by these people for reasons of creating a Bible in the newly-named language!

The city of Ile-Ife is considered by the Yoruba to be the seat of creation. The paramount chief of Ife, called the Oni of Ife, is thought of as the spiritual head of all the Yoruba. As Yoruba religion underwent all the necessary adaptations in order to survive in the hostile Cuban environment, eventually becoming known as Santería, Ife became less and less relevant. The Orisha, however, continued to be of utmost importance. To this day, millions of Cubans, Brazilians, and, increasingly, people of all races and ethnic backgrounds, depend on the wise counsel of these African divinities to make it through an increasingly harsh modern world. After our brief meandering through the origins of Orisha worship, Let us return to our exposition on the Divine Ferryman, Aganjú, who helped steer his devotees to survival in the New World.

Aganjú's mother is the fearsome Oro Ainá, the molten lava which forms a volcano when it erupts through the crust of the Earth. This molten rock, semi-solid fire, transforms into very rich soil when it cools down, thus giving birth to the wilderness, an area rich with plant life and animals. As the son of Oro Ainá, Aganjú is represented in the opening that allows Mother Earth to release her pressure. He, then, can be thought of as the gate keeper that gives Oro Ainá the ability to release her anger, the mediator that helps his mother express her awesome power. Aganjú is the mouth and throat of the world. As the gate keeper for the mysteries of the inner Earth, Aganjú is to be given a high place among the divinities (Orisha) which make up Santería's pantheon.

Aganjú's role as a mediator is further developed in his capacity as the ferryman who takes souls from the material to the spiritual plane after they experience death. A ferryman has to know the river he travels very well; he must chart the safest course and keep his passengers out of harm's way. In this fashion, Aganjú personifies the wise guide who takes people to new places, the teacher who tells his students that sometimes the greatest blessings come out of overcoming great obstacles.

As the personification of the wilderness, Aganjú exemplifies the lone wolf, the man or woman who is drawn to the great outdoors, cherishing the opportunity to commune with nature.

Because of his great age and physical prowess, Aganjú is generally thought of as wielding enormous power. Aganjú is one of a group of Orisha called the "ancient ones." Some African theologians go as far as to say that Aganjú does not represent the more recent generation of supernatural beings called "Orisha," but belongs to an older race of Great Ones called the "irunmole." These irunmole, vis-a-vis the Orisha, hold a position analogous to that of the great titans of ancient Greece in relation to the gods of Mount Olympus. In Santería, however, Aganjú is considered a powerful Orisha, one so powerful that his ashe is not implanted directly on the heads of his priests. Although some people in Cuba received the priesthood of Aganjú directly, in most instances it was either Shangó or Yemaya that served as a bridge to the more awesome Aganjú.[2]

A salient exception to priests who followed the custom of not installing Aganjú directly on an initiate's head was the erudite priest of Shangó Nicolas Angarica, author of one of the most widely read Santería manuals, who clearly expounds on how he became the first Santero to install Aganjú directly on the head in Havana. Angarica said he learned the secrets associated with such a ceremony from the legendary Oba Dimeji, a glorious figure in Cuban Santería.

ORO AINA Terrifying Mother of Aganju

There seems to be some confusion between the primordial Orisha Aganjú, who inhabited the Earth untold eons ago, and Oba Aganjú, who ruled as emperor of Oyo in relatively modern times. To make matters even more confusing, both Aganjús have a strong connection to someone named Shangó. In the case of the ancient Orisha, Shangó was his junior. In the case of the historical Aganjú, he was the nephew of the fourth king of Oyo, Shangó, who probably lived a thousand years ago. [3] A way to make some sense out of this confusion is to apply concepts found in the branch of Hinduism called "Bhakti Yoga," specifically Vaishnava Bhakti (devotion to Vishnu), to Santería.

Bhakti Yoga teaches that God (Vishnu) descends to Earth from his heavenly abode from time to time, whenever there is a great need for his compassion, taking on a material body. These incarnations of God are called "avatars." Using this model, the historical Shangó and Aganjú, then, may be thought of as avatars of the older deities.

The reason why such contradictions do not bother Africans as much as they do Cubans is that people raised in Yoruba traditional culture, the source of Cuban Santería, did not believe their gods were subjected to linear time. They were thought to exist in what they called "spiral time." Under this concept, parallel histories of the same entities can exist side by side without causing much concern to the believers, who accept that the Orisha need not be subjected to natural laws, thus, in some stories Shangó is the son of Aganjú and Yemaya, in others he is the son of Aganjú and Oshanlá, while in others Shangó is not Aganjú's son at all, but his uncle! As the nephew and successor of the historical Shangó, the historical Aganjú was a great Alafin (king) of Oyo. In his *History of the Yoruba,* Samuel Johnson writes: His *reign was long and very prosperous. He had a remarkable faculty of taming wild animals and venomous reptiles, several of which may be seen crawling about him. He had also in his house a tame leopard.'*

As Johnson goes on to state, however, Alafin Aganjú had a tragic end. His favorite son and heir had an illicit affair with Aganjú's favorite wife. According to Yoruba tradition, all of one's father's wives are to be considered one's "mothers." Because his fault was considered incest, the prince was condemned to death. Oba Aganjú died shortly afterwards of a broken heart.

Aganju and Oshanla

1

Sacred Stories About Aganjú

One of the most often-told stories about Aganjú in Santería concerns his encounter with a disguised Oshanlá.[5] It is said that the great mother goddess, Oshanlá, decided to have some fun at the expense of the irascible and taciturn old man of the river, Aganjú. Disguising herself as a peasant woman, Oshanlá boarded the ferry owned by Aganjú which he used to carry people and cargo from one side of the River Oshún to the other. Aganjú was known for not allowing anyone to cross on his boat unless he got paid. After crossing the river, all passengers paid their fare to Aganjú except for the handsome peasant woman whom he had observed laughing most of the time it took to cross the river.

Becoming enraged, Aganjú shouted, "No man or woman laughs at Aganjú! You pay me my fare or I'll throw you in the river, woman!" Softly laughing, the mysterious beauty of indecipherable age fell to her knees and, extending bare arms of an incredibly soft brown color towards Aganjú, she motioned for him to join her by the river bank. "Come, don't be angry, I have no money, but I can pay you with some loving." Although not used to this peculiar method of collecting his fare, Aganjú could not resist the beguiling invitation. Putting her clothes back on after an intense love-making session, the beautiful peasant woman left Aganjú's embrace, still softly laughing. After the experience, Aganjú thought of no one but the mysterious woman, longing for her kisses, hoping to see her again.

Oshanla tells Aganju that Shango is their son

Nine months later Oshanlá gave birth to a beautiful baby boy she named Shangó. Ashamed of what she had done, Oshanlá gave the child to her daughter Yemaya to raise as her own. The Orisha of the sea raised the boy with much love, never telling him who his real parents were. Shangó grew up to be a strapping youth, so sinewy and beautiful that all who saw him felt a tinge of excitement within their hearts. As the boy grew older, he demanded to know who his father was. Not being able to remain silent anymore, Yemaya told the boy. "Your real mother is Oshanlá, my beloved Iya (mother). Go ask her who your father is." Presenting himself to the grand empress he always thought was his grandmother, Shangó demanded to know the truth. Since Oshanlá prided herself in her candor, she told Shangó where to find his father. "Go to the edge of the Oshún river, there by a great campfire at night you will meet your destiny. But before you go, I must grant you a special boon, that is, that nothing your father does to you will be able to harm a hair on your head!"

Arriving at the river, Shangó noticed a great hulk of a man relaxing by the shore, next to a great bonfire. Although obviously much older than Shangó, the man's body was equally beautiful. The young man immediately recognized in the lone stranger the author of his days. Waiting in the shadows until Aganjú fell asleep, Shangó surreptitiously grabbed a rabbit that was cooking in Aganjú's fire, stealing it and then eating it. When the old Orisha woke up and saw a young man eating his dinner, he demanded to know what was going on. "I am your son Shangó, I deserve to eat of your dinner." Opening his eyes wide and gritting his ax-strong teeth, Aganjú shouted: "I HAVE NO CHILDREN!" He then proceeded to pound on the boy with fierce strength. Much to his surprise, Shangó just stood there as if nothing had happened. "You must be an ajogun (demon) sent here to test me, I don't care, I can kill you with my fire." Aganjú then punched two holes in the earth next to where Shangó stood, two springs of molten lava then jumped on the young man until he was buried under a mountain of red-hot semi-liquid rock. With great aplomb, Shangó shook the lava off his person as if it were dandruff. "Come on, father, stop playing games," Shangó said. Not knowing what else to do, Aganjú threw Shangó into the bonfire, from where he emerged unscathed. "It must be true, then. You must really come from my loins, for only the son of Aganjú could walk away from inside a fire, but who is your mother?" At that moment the Empress Oshanlá appeared, wearing her royal robes. Aganjú fell on his face, offering his queen full obeisance. "I am the mother, Aganjú." Still facing the floor, Aganjú protested "My Lady, how can you say that? This your servant has never disrespected you in any way!" Turning herself into the peasant woman Aganjú had pined for during the last eighteen years,

Aganjú pummels Shangó

she saw the old man's eyes fill with tears when he realized the great goddess had played a trick on him. "Do not feel bad, Aganjú, things happen as they happen and we are all actors in the continuing drama of life. Now here is your son and he needs you to teach him how to be a man." Oshanlá then left the two, who had the hard task ahead of them of learning to know each other.

Aganjú watches as Shangó
emerges from the flames unscathed

Commentary: As with many other sacred stories in Santería, the divinities here are shown having flawed characters. Since the Orisha are to be understood as personified and diverse aspects of the one transcendental Divinity, Olodumare, it is logical to assume that their apparent foibles are to be looked at from a different perspective one would view human foibles. In India this "past-time of the gods" is called "lila." Just as an Indian devotee understands Lord Krishna's many sexual escapades with married cowgirls ("gopis") as encompassing some very deep lessons on the nature of Divine Love, one who worships the Orisha should strive to find the higher lessons contained in these apparently ribald parables.

This story of Aganjú and Oshanlá is unusual in that it even portrays the Great Mother, Oshanlá, usually depicted as a paragon of virtue, as being less than pure. In fact, not only does she commit adultery in the story, but she also gives up the baby which resulted from her adulterous dalliance to her daughter Yemaya, keeping the child in the dark about who his father was for eighteen years!

The underlying lesson in this story is that order and balance must be maintained at all costs. The solidity of Aganjú's "lava" had to merge with the ethereal coolness of Oshanlá's womb for the birth of gaseous fire, Shangó, to occur.

Although Oshanlá is shown as being uncharacteristically saucy in this story, Aganjú's character as a taciturn, stubborn, dogged and rugged individualist is consistent with depictions of him found in Africa and throughout the Diaspora.

In his popular book *El Santo: La Ocha* *Julio* Garcia Cortez tells an interesting variation on the Aganjú-as-father-of-Shangó theme. Since I have never encountered this particular story in Cuba, but had heard it when I traveled in Africa, I assume Cortez must have come across it there also. In this story, Aganjú's often alluded-to, but seldom explained closeness to Oshún is expressed.

As this story goes, a great drought encompassed the earth and no one, not even Olofi God, knew where all the water had gone. Eshu was sent on a mission to find it. After searching for many days, Eshu found a great stream. Thirstily throwing himself in the rolling waters, Eshu was shocked to feel a great wallop of a punch throwing him several feet away. Not seeing who punched him, Eshu tried again to approach the stream. This time he barely caught glimpse of a blur that pushed him away with enormous force. "I am Eshu and I come from Olofi, I demand to know who has pushed me away." A giant of a man, almost seven feet tall, appeared in front of Eshu. Obviously of mature age, he nevertheless appeared to be in excellent physical condition. "I am Aganjú and these are my waters." "Forgive my intrusion, Great One," Eshu told the man. "The entire world thirsts,Olofi will give you whatever you desire, but you must allow your fellow creatures to share your water, or we'll all die!" Without hesitating, Aganjú said: "I will supply the three worlds with water, all I want is Oshún's hand in marriage." The gorgeous maiden Oshún was Olofi's favorite daughter. With a wave of Aganjú's hand, one hundred-one horses appeared carrying many goat skins filled with water. "Take this small offering to Father Olofi so he sees that I am serious." When little Eshu arrived in town followed by a hundred and one horses carrying thousands of gallons of water, the whole populace rejoiced and hailed him as a hero. Eshu then told Olofi what Aganjú wanted. Oshún heard what Eshu said, and immediately agreed to marry Aganjú. Olofi consented. "He is not a youngster, my princess, but he is a very handsome man. I think you will not be disappointed with him," Eshu told the beautiful damsel. At that moment, a torrential rain began to fall, everyone went outside their abodes to celebrate the water. Oshún also went out, but the rains became so rough that she could hardly see in front of her. She said out loud "Where should I go?" and a voice said "Here!" She followed the voice until she found herself inside a luxurious castle. Eerily, there was no one around, but things looked extremely well cared for. Oshún realized this must be the realm of her mysterious husband. At night she felt as if someone was making love to her, but when she awoke, there would be no one there. In the morning she'd get up to find a sumptuous breakfast waiting for her. Later she'd find her robes all washed and dried, her meals prepared, and her bed freshly made, but she'd never see anyone. Oshún soon discovered she was pregnant. Talking out loud she said "Oh, how I wish I could have this child with my kin, back in my town!" A voice said "You shall!" Oshún then looked around to find herself in the familiar quarters of her compound, back in her father's house. Received with great joy, she told her father about her strange circumstances. Olofi felt sad for his daughter, but Aganjú had kept his end of their bargain and he found no fault with him, although he wished his mysterious son-in-law would behave more normally.

When her baby was born, Oshún named him Shangó. She then knew it was time to return to her invisible husband. "I wish I could take my hand maiden with me to keep me company!" A voice was heard, "You may!" Oshún and her hand maiden, Senia, then found themselves in the ghostly castle. As Oshún would take walks and meditate by the river, trying to make sense of her strange life—she was even beginning to feel love for her phantom husband—she would leave Shangó under the care of Senia. Unfortunately, Senia was beginning to react to the eerie ambiance to which she was being subjected by taking it out on the baby, hitting him when he cried and calling him a "son without a father." One day Oshún walked in when Senia was abusing the baby, she opened her mouth to curse Senia, but much to her surprise, an extremely tall, good-looking man dressed in royal finery appeared from nowhere. "How dare you insult my son! Oshún,

Aganjú, Oshún, and baby Shangó

send this woman back to her town, from now on you shall have all the hand maidens, cooks, butlers, and anything else you want!" Right in front of her eyes, Oshún began to see people appear, looking out the window, Oshún saw a bustling town, full of life. "This is our realm, my wife, we remain invisible to those we wish to ignore, but from now on you and our son will rule alongside me!" Garcia Cortez mentions that when elders finish telling this story, they'll say: "Never call a child a bastard, or a single mother a loose woman."

Although depictions of Aganjú may vary somewhat from community to community, his relationship to Oro Ainá (the Fiery Mother) and his dominion of the river as a tough navigator who ferries people to safety appears to be constant.

Like most loners, Aganjú teaches by example rather than in a didactic fashion. As the mediator of an awesome natural force, the volcano, Aganjú represents the overcoming of great, unavoidable obstacles. As a navigator, he exemplifies the need for careful planning. As a ferryman between worlds, Aganjú represents growth, both spiritual and mental. He also epitomizes the potentialities present in unavoidable change. Aganjú also represents freedom from bondage and in such a capacity was not only highly venerated in Cuba during slave times, but was identified publicly with the Catholic St. Christopher, patron saint of Havana.

According to Roman Martyrology, Christopher's birth name was Offerus, the son of a heathen king. It is said that Offerus grew to over seven feet tall. He decided to put himself at the service of the most powerful man on earth. He first served a king said to be the most potent in the world, but the king was terrified of the Devil. Offerus then sought out the Devil, only to find out that Satan was afraid of Christ. He then declared his allegiance to Christ, in time he became the disciple of a hermit who told him he should give himself in service to Christ. The hermit baptized Offerus, changing his name to Christopher, (Christ bearer). Christopher, though now a "Christian" would not fast or pray. He took up the task of carrying people across a raging stream as his duty to Christ. One day he was carrying a child across the stream and the child grew heavier as they crossed the stream, until it seemed to Christopher that he was carrying the weight of the world on his shoulders. The Child revealed himself to be the creator and redeemer of the world. To prove that he was who he said he was, the child told Christopher to stick his wooden staff into the earth and leave it there. The next day it was a palm tree full of fruit. Upon seeing this Christopher became a zealous Christian and traveled about preaching the Gospel of Jesus Christ. On a trip to Lycia, which is in modern day Iran, his first sermon caused eight thousand of the locals to request baptism. (Saint Christopher is the Patron of travelers) When Emperor Decius got word of this. He commanded that Christopher be arrested, tortured and beheaded. Saint Christopher's day is celebrated on July 25th.

Natalia Bolivar Arostegui, the greatest living recorder of Afro-Cuban life, says that she considers the syncretism of Aganjú with Saint Christopher very natural. Both exhibit great physical prowess, both agree to transport people across a river, and both are represented as having a close connection with the palm tree.

Aganjú is also syncretized with Saint Joseph, who according to the Catholic Church is of royal lineage, the husband of the Virgin, and the patron saint of Church. His feast day is March 19; with Saint John the Evangelist, one of the first of the Apostles who stood in support of Mary by the cross during the crucifixion; and with St. Peter, custodian of Heaven's Gates. In the easternmost part of Cuba, in the city of Santiago, Aganjú is identified with St. Michael the Archangel, Captain of the armies of God, whose battle cry is: *Mi Ka El* (Who is like God?). His feast day is September 29.

It is said that Aganjú's hour is sunrise, for he is thought to be one with the sun. This association with the rising sun makes Aganjú an Orisha people seek when they need hope, when they literally need to experience the dawn of a new day.

2
ATTRIBUTES

Necklace

Aganjú's necklace is made by alternating nine dark brown beads with nine soapy white ones, and interpolating in equidistant spaces four brightly colored beads such as red, blue, green, and yellow. A simpler necklace is made by alternating one brown, one soapy white, one brown etc., until the desired length is achieved.

Shrine (igbodu)—How initiates honor Aganjú[6]

In merindilogun divination, Aganjú speaks through Osa (nine shells). Nicolas Angarica claims Aganjú also speaks in Irosun (four shells). His emblematic color is very dark red, the color of dried blood. His number is nine. His representative vessel for initiates is usually an earthenware or terra cotta pot, sometimes painted in nine different colors, where his initiatory tools are stored. These include three or nine iron implements—a knife, a sword, an ax etc., sixteen mate seeds, and a large stone in the shape of a mount. Aganjú is worshipped by lighting nine pieces of cotton twisted into wicks and drenched in palm oil.

Shrine (olujo alejo)—How non-initiates may begin to honor Aganjú

Non-initiates who want to honor Aganjú but have no access to elders who can help them with their altar can set up a temporary shrine as a focus of their devotion featuring nine volcanic rocks, a dark-red or brown candle, a small terra cotta dish filled with water, and an iron table food warmer, the kind used in Chinese restaurants; they make great fire offerings to

Aganjú, better than just a candle. Just please make sure you leave no fire unattended. If you don't mind Catholic iconography, you may include a picture of St. Christopher in your shrine.

Bombo de Aganjú: My Madrina, Amanda Gomez Ochalache, devised a particularly efficient way of meditating on the Orisha of volcanoes, with the use of a *reberbero,* a kind of portable cast iron mini-furnace such as one sees in Chinese restaurants, where these little cookers are placed right on the tables so that patrons can keep their hors d'oeuvres warm. Amanda would put a small piece of cotton drenched in alcohol inside the small (about as large as a cup) cast-iron cooker, lighting it up with a match. She would then sit in front of the *Bombo* meditating on Aganjú, offering the flames to the god of liquid fire. Amanda taught all of her godchildren how to make these little bombos[7], a practice she said she learned from a Dahomeian priestess of Saborissa who had been one of her teachers. I have personally taught many of my own godchildren how to work with a bombo, and I find it a very satisfying—and safe—way to honor fire, as well as Aganjú.

Offerings (adimu): He accepts all fruits and has a fondness for eggplants and crackers dressed with palm oil—nine at a time. According to famed santero Nicolas Angarica, Aganjú enjoys mashed, boiled, green plantains (fu fu), okra and beef shortrib stew.

Blood offerings (ebd): In earlier times, bulls were sacrificed for Aganjú. Nowadays castrated goats seem to be the most serious offerings made to the Orisha. Other offerings given to Aganjú include roosters, pigeons, quails and guinea fowl.

Characteristics of Aganjú (and of his devotees): Aganjú's Catholic disguise in Cuba is St. Christopher, his feast day is July 25th. In Dilogun, he speaks through the following *letras* (chapters): Osa (9 shells up), Irosun (4), and Okana (1).

Nicolas Angarica says that Aganjú represents the sun and the volcano, the sun because of his vastness, the volcano because of his devastating strength. Aganjú is also the Divine ferryman, an Orisha who helps his devotees in times of transition, such as a soul must undergo when leaving an earthly existence towards a spiritual plane. Aganjú's representation as a ferryman is allegorical to his character as the Orisha who acts as arbiter when elders make mistakes; the one who "steers them right" through troubled waters. If a Baba or an Iya installs the wrong Orisha on an initiate's head, Aganjú is invoked to act as that priesthood holder's advocate. He is thought to make things right with a minimum of embarrassment for the erring priest or priestess. Angarica also says that Aganjú speaks through Osa (9 shells up) because he embodies the nine necessary elements of life: Light, fire, water, soil, air, food, health, wealth, and birth.[8] Lydia Cabrera calls Aganjú " The owner of the wilderness, of the heavens, and of the rainbow. He is the Strong Man, the one with the power."[9] Scholar and Orisha priest Carlos Canet says that in the city of Ondo, in modem Nigeria, Aganjú is worshipped as a fertility god, and his help is sought by barren women who wish to conceive.[10]

When priests of the fiery Orisha are possessed by Aganjú—not a common occurrence—they jump very high and take long, exaggerated steps as they walk. When Aganjú mounts his devotees, he is known to pick up babies and small children, carrying them on his shoulders in order to give them blessings. Children of Aganjú—as those people who are guarded by the Orisha from the moment of their birth are called—tend to be quick-tempered, even violent. Aganjú's children also tend to be physically powerful. They love children and are "suckers" for hard-luck stories. Male children of Aganjú are said to be particularly vulnerable to fragile looking con-women seemingly in need of protection. All children of Aganjú should wear a red sash around their waists, under their clothes. Aganjú has dominion over fevers and high blood pressure. He is said, like Ogun, to be able to protect his devotees from automobile accidents.

ROADS OF AGANJÚ:

In the Cuban tradition, Aganjú is rarely installed directly in his initiate's head. Instead, the mysteries that are actually presented to the heads of his priests and priestesses belong either to Shangó or to Yemaya, this last one thought to have been his wife in one of her avatars. All initiates whose Orisha parents are Shangó and Oshún have to receive Aganjú as well.

John Mason has said that Aganjú is important to the growth of civilization in that he hurdles physical obstacles and opens uncharted geographic and psychological frontiers, therefore stimulating cosmopolitanism and allowing people to look at new realities; this being the reason for Aganjú's reputation as one who can do the impossible, one who can overcome the greatest obstacles.

Some of the roads (avatars) or manifestations of Aganjú include the following:

Aganjú Sola (Awasoda): The ferryman.
Aganjú Kiniba (or Kinini Oba): An old and royal avatar. "The Careful and Accurate King."
Aganjú Obadina (or Oninfi): volcanic manifestation. Lord of Lava. Probably an ancient manifestation, for there are no active volcanoes anywhere near Yorubaland or Cuba.

Aganjú Aggari (Aganjú Aged, Aganjú Lan): The wilderness personified, the name literally means "obstinate wilderness." In *El Monte,* Lydia Cabrera says that Aganjú Aggari is "A very ancient Aganjú."
Oro Ina: Sometimes thought to be a separate Orisha (his mother), or a female form of Aganjú. The fiery core of the earth.
Saborissa: Arara name for Aganjú.
Brazo fuerte: Palo name for Aganjú

Cleansings:

Many cleansings with Aganjú involve the use of fire. These should be left to experts. A simple cleansing to get rid of bad luck that can be done safely by anyone is to take nine large salty (not sweet) crackers, or nine soda crackers, dress them with palm oil, light a nine-day dark red or brown candle to Aganjú and leave the offering on a plate for nine days. After nine days, put spent candle, including glass, crackers, and even the plate, inside a paper bag, pass paper bag with contents all over your body as you mentally ask Aganjú to cleanse you, then leave bag with contents at the foot of a large tree in a park or woodsy area. Choose a spot you don't frequent much.

Respected Cuban elder Nicolas Angarica says that Aganjú is *okanini* (of one heart) with Oya. Because of this, he can be offered nine small eggplants as an adimu, after nine days the person can then clean himself/herself spiritually by passing the nine eggplants all over his/her body and throwing out the offering, along with nine pennies, by the gate of a cemetery. The fact that Aganjú is close to Oya can be gleaned in the fact that both speak through dilogun by the same *letra, Osa* (nine shells up), and both share the deep red/brown colored necklaces interspersed with multicolored beads.

Herbs and plants: Sarsaparilla, china berry, and peepal trees belong to Aganjú.

Dilogun letra: Osa (9 shells up)

3

AGANJÚ AND SANTERIA'S "CELESTIAL COURT"

In Africa, Orisha worshippers generally belong to a society ("egbe") dedicated to the worship of a single Orisha, thus, worshippers of Aganjú would belong to egbe Aganjú, those who worship Yemaya would belong to egbe Yemaya and so forth. These societies were in fact denominations, fully self-sufficient and not necessarily having anything to do with initiations into Orishas other than their own. The three elements of Orisha worship that transcended the boundaries of egbe were Eshu worship, ancestor veneration ("egungun") and Ha divination. Eshu was worshipped across the board because, as the Orisha who opens and closes doors, both literal and metaphysical, he could keep anyone from achieving anything. The ancestors, of course, form the backbone of most indigenous spiritualities, for it is in great part deified ancestors who receive the greatest amount of worship in many of these primal societies. Ha priests have attained great fame and respect as codifiers, recorders, and teachers of Orisha worship. Although strictly speaking they are one more egbe among many, in reality they are the scholars of Orisha worship and have attained the status of high priests.

During the shameful days of the slave trade, members of all egbes were criminally brought to the Americas. Due to the horrible conditions endured by these incredibly brave men, women and children, they found their lives interrupted in a fashion so lacking in humanity it is hard for us today to imagine our ancestors being subjected to such ignominy just a few generations ago. Members of different egbes would be grouped together in different plantations. Lacking the infrastructures they had enjoyed in their homeland, egbes that in Africa would have nothing to do with each other became associated by necessity. A member of egbe Oshún, for example, would teach a member of egbe Aganjú about his religion, while the member of Aganjú's egbe would reciprocate. In this fashion, each worshipper made sure his or her Orisha would not fall into oblivion. Eventually, a synthesis began to occur where the egbes began to become fused into a single religion, Lukumi, also called "Regla de Ocha" and Santeria.

Where the ashe of a single Orisha would be revealed to an initiate in Africa, a standard five Orisha were offered automatically in a Santeria initiation, though only one of these would be installed in a person's head. The five standard Orishas were: Eshu (Eleggua), Obatala, Shangó, Yemaya, and Oshún. Apparently not enough members of egbe Aganjú arrived in Cuba to keep his initiation popular, for very few houses in Cuba directly initiate people into Aganjú's mysteries.

All houses, however, venerate Aganjú as part of the family of Shangó, another Orisha of fire and water, and Yemaya, enormously popular Orisha of the sea. It is through these two Orisha that the ashe of Aganjú is usually implanted in a neophyte's psyche.

Cuban elders refer to the Santeria pantheon as "La Corte Celestial," the Celestial Court. Aganjú's position in the pantheon is very important because of his close association with the extremely popular Shangó. As those who know the secret of installing Aganjú's ashe directly become more willing to share their precious knowledge, Aganjú's cult can only become greater.

4

ORIKI AGANJÚ;
ORIN AGANJÚ

PRAYERS AND SONGS TO AGANJÚ

Those who have been initiated as priests and priestesses in Santeria can increase the power of cleansings and works they do with Aganjú by reciting praise verses called "oriki" and by singing praise songs called "orin" in Lukumi that have been in use in Cuba for hundreds of years.

Speakers of standard Yoruba have no trouble recognizing the meaning of the Lukumi words.

Oriki
Aganjú sola mi'o
Aganjú, ferryman, Lord of the Waters
Aganjú sola mi'o
Aganjú, ferryman, Lord of the Waters
Baba nya se re'ko
Father overflows to cover the crops

Orin

Aganjú Sola Tanile? 'Ni'yo Eyo un
Is Aganjú the master of the house?
He owns all the money he could want.

Oya, Oya, Takua Oya[12]
With Oya, Oya, from the Takua (nupe) Oya

Orin

Ishu La Te Re Re Aganjú Te Re Re
We offer Aganjú yam and okra, may he give us Grace.

Omiran Ishu Le Le Aya Te Re Re
May your wife who is like a great yam give us grace.

Ishu La Te Re Re Aganjú Te Le Omiran
We offer Aganjú yam and okra, may the great giant give us grace.

Ma Ma Shoro Shoro Aganjú Shoro Shoro
Verily verily you are fierce, Aganjú, you are most fierce.

Orin

Lead
Eleku ee, eleku ee, eleku ee
The owner of the cave, the owner of the cave

Aganjú eleku e aye
Aganjú is the owner of the cave in the world

Chorus
Eleku ee, eleku ee, eleku ee
The owner of the cave, the owner of the cave

Aganjú eleku e aye
Aganjú is the owner of the cave in the world

Lead
Repeat verse

Chorus
Repeat verse

Lead
Repeat verse

Chorus
Repeat verse

Lead
Omoba tele, olube o
The prince walks the earth, the prince walks the earth

Omoba tele, Aganjú omoba tele
The prince walks the earth, the wilderness, the prince walks
the earth

Eni alado, oni Sango
He who owns the medicine gourd, the possessor of Sango

Omoba tele, so koto
The prince walks the earth, the wizard of the deep vessel

Chorus   **Omoba tele, omaba tele**
The prince walks the earth, the prince walks the earth

Omoba tele, omaba tele
The prince walks the earth, the prince walks the earth

Eni alado, oni Sango
He who owns the medicine gourd, the possessor of Sango

Omoba tele, so koto
The prince walks the earth, the wizard of the deep vessel

Lead   **Omoba tele, olube o**
The prince walks the earth, the prince walks the earth

Omoba tele, Aganjú omoba tele
The prince walks the earth, the wilderness, the prince
walks the earth

Eni alado, oni Sango
He who owns the medicine gourd, the possessor of Sango

Omoba tele, so koto
The prince walks the earth, the wizard of the deep vessel

Omoba tele, omaba tele
The prince walks the earth, the prince walks the earth

Chorus   **Omoba tele, omaba tele**
The prince walks the earth, the prince walks the earth

Eni alado, oni Sango
He who owns the medicine gourd, the possessor of Sango

Omoba tele, so koto
The prince walks the earth, the wizard of the deep vessel

Lead

Tele' moba tele' moba, tele Aganjú, tele (e)'le
Follow after the prince, follow after the prince.
Follow after Aganjú, follow after power.

Chorus

Tele' moba tele' moba, tele
Follow after the prince, follow

Lead

Aganjú, tele (e)'le
Aganjú, follow after power.

Chorus

Tele' moba tele' moba, tele
Follow after the prince, follow

Lead

Aganjú, tele (e)'le
Aganjú, follow after power.

Chorus

Tele' moba tele' moba, tele
Follow after the prince, follow

Lead

Aganjú, tele (e)'le
Aganjú, follow after power.

Chorus

Tele' moba tele' moba, tele
Follow after the prince, follow

Lead

Ma, ma ma so ro so aye
Do not, do not, do not shoot up to drop with a crash to earth

Aganjú so ro so
The wilderness shoots up to drop with a crash to earth

Ma, ma ma so ro so aye
Do not, do not, do not shoot up to drop with a crash to earth

Aganjú so ro so
The wilderness shoots up to drop with a crash to earth

Ma, ma ma so ro so aye
Do not, do not, do not shoot up to drop with a crash to earth

Aganjú so ro so
The wilderness shoots up to drop with a crash to earth

5

DESPOJOS/CLEANSINGS
WITH AGANJÚ

According to Yoruba tradition, when a subject makes a meal that pleases the monarch, the king is obliged to offer the subject a reward. Since Aganjú, like Shangó, is considered the epitome of a Yoruba monarch, he enjoys conferring boons on those devotees who cook his favorite food for him: *fu fu*. To this day *fu fu*, called mofongo in Puerto Rico and Santo Domingo, is a delicacy in the Spanish-speaking Caribbean. The following is the recipe for *fu fu* that has been passed down in my family from generation to generation. Remember when cooking for the Orisha that you are not to partake of the food with them—all of it is to be deposited in an appropriate place. In the case of Aganjú, at the foot of a large tree or, sometimes, in a river. The hard working Aganjú will more than likely grant your requests after he has enjoyed an offering of some good *fu fu!*

FU FU DE PLATANO FOR AGANJÚ

Ingredients
three very green plantains
4 ounces of cut-up pork meat
lard
one small onion
one clove garlic

Peel the plantain, which must be very green outside and cream colored inside. Cut into two-inch wheels, boil for about half-an-hour. While plantains are boiling. Peel and dice onion and garlic, mix with pork meat, which had been cut into small pieces. Fry meat, onion, and garlic in three tablespoons of lard until well cooked, about fifteen minutes over medium heat. Set aside fried meat. Take boiled pieces of plantain and, using a mortar and pestle, reduce to a paste. Put some of the grease from the meat in a tall bowl or large cup, using your hands, press the plantain paste into the bowl, then turn over so when you remove the bowl, the fu fu retains the bowl's shape. Now put meat and more grease on top as a garnish. Is it any wonder Aganjú just loves this dish! I recommend that at least sometimes you do this exclusively for Aganjú. If, however, you wish to make *fu fu* in honor of Aganjú but also serve some to family and friends, then take his portion out first, and do not put salt on the food until the Orisha's portion has been taken out. Remember that the Orisha and the Egun prefer their food without salt.

DESPOJO DE LOS NUEVE DIAS: AGANJÚ'S NINE DAY CLEANSING

Ingredients
a dark brown nine-day candle
nine pennies
a branch from a China Berry tree
two coconuts

Before you start any cleansing, ask Eleggua's favor by offering him twenty-one cents and some candy at a crossroads. Start this cleansing on a Thursday at noon and repeat the following instructions for a period of nine days. Place the candle by an altar to Aganjú or, if you do not have one, place it where it will not be disturbed. Light the candle and present the branch of China Berry to Aganjú by saying "Ago Aganjú, Funmini Re!" then proceed to strike all walls of your place of residence with the branch. Leave the branch by the candle, along with one penny each day at midday. On the ninth day, after you leave your ninth penny by the offering, take two coconuts and, using your right foot, roll them all over your house—you can have a second person help you by rolling one while you roll the other. After you are through, present the coconuts to Aganjú by the candle while saying "Modupue, Babami, Kawo, Omiran!" Now turn off the candle, if it hasn't already turned off by itself, and take all ingredients, including candle and pennies, as well as the tree branch, and put them inside a bag. Proceed to a river, and throw it in as far as you can. Your household and your aura will be equally cleared by this potent cleansing.

AN EBO TO ENSURE PROSPERITY

This particular ebo comes from the Xango-Aganjú Umbandista house in Brazil. Gather the following ingredients.

nine non-sweet crackers

palm oil (manteca de corojo)

nine small (finger) candles, brown

nine pennies

Nine small tumbled stones, the kind cheaply bought at places where they sell semi-precious and exotic crystals.

A piece of reddish-brown cloth three feet square

This ebo requires that you set apart each day for nine days a time to perform the necessary operation-preferably at nine each morning. Before you begin the operation, make sure you have a clear and strong impression of the kind of wealth you want to achieve. The first day, set up an altar by opening the cloth, placing the shiny stones on top, spreading some palm oil on each of the crackers, and lighting the first candle. As the candle burns, visualize the wealth you want and ask Aganjú as the king of Oyo to grant it to you, after about 20 minutes, snuff out the candle, leave it there, along with a penny. The next day, light up another candle, again meditate on wealth from Aganjú for twenty minutes, snuff out the second candle, adding it to the first, as well as adding a second penny. On the third day, again light a new candle, meditate, add a penny. On the ninth day, after you add the ninth candle and ninth penny to the ebo, make a bundle by tying everything inside the reddish-brown cloth and take it to the foot of a large *ceiba* (silk cotton tree), or any other very large tree if there are no ceibas where you live. Within 21 days you will see your economy improve.

AN EBO TO RESTORE A FEVER SUFFERER'S HEALTH

Ingredients
Live chicken
Nine potatoes
Three plantains
Palm oil

If a person appears to be suffering from a persistent fever, sacrifice a chicken to Aganjú, prepare the chicken for cooking. You may use dry spices to flavor chicken, but no salt. Place chicken in large pot, add nine small peeled potatoes, three peeled plantains, cut in four parts each, and two tablespoonfuls of palm oil. Fill pot with water. Boil everything for two hours. Make sure no one tastes resulting soup until after it has been offered to Aganjú for his blessing by placing pot full of cooked soup in front of a representation of Aganjú-his pot or an image of a saint representing him. After a few minutes, serve a bowl full of soup to the sick person. He should eat as much as he can. His fever will be gone.

volcano

[1] See Dr. Yosef BenJochannan, "Another Dimension of Zulu Christianity," *The Long Search,* (Dubuque, Iowa: Kendall-Hunt Publishing, 1978), Pp.56-57.

[2] Priesthood holders in my lineage have always installed Aganjú directly. The ceremonies we use at present were handwritten by Ferminita Gomez in the 1930's. Many of her descendants own Xerox copies of her original notes.

[3] Although some scholars place Shangó's reign as recently as the 1500's c.e., Wande Abimbola in his book Ifa Will *Mend Our Broken World* (Roxbury, Mass: Aim Books, 1997) states that Shangó reigned more than 1000 years ago.

[4] Samuel Johnson, *The History ojthe Yoruba,* (Lagos, Nigeria: CMS Bookshops, 1921;1960), p. 155.

[5] Sometimes "Yemmu" is named instead of "Oshanlá." Since "Oshanlá" means "the Great Orisha," both sources may be referring to the same deity by different names.

[6] As the learned priest of Obatala John Mason has noted, Aganjú's character as a loner who inhabits the desolate wilderness is mirrored in the custom, common in Cuba, of setting up Aganjú's altar by himself, away from other Orisha. See Mason, *Orin Orisa,* (Brooklyn: Y.T.A., 1992), p. 190.

[7] Amanda would dress the little iron pot with palm oil, later washing it with omiero from Aganjú's shrine, while singing three suyeres to Aganjú. She would then confer these little bombos on people whom she thought needed to be connected to Fire for some reason.

[8] See *Angarica,Manual del Orihate: Religion Lucumi* (Havana: Self-Published, 1955) p. 51. A bootleg version of this book is widely available, an English -language version of the Spanish-language bootleg now being offered in the internet!

[9] Lydia Cabrera, *La Laguna Sagrada de San Joaquin,* (Madrid: Editorial "R", 1973), p.89.

[10] Carlos Canet, *Lucumi: Religion de los Yoruba en Cuba* (Miami: Editorial A.I.P., 1973), p.64.

[11] Lydia Cabrera, El *Monie* (Miami: Editora Universal, 1976), p. 235.

[12] In his book Ija Will *Mend Our Broken World* (Roxbury, Mass: Aim Books, 1997), page 147, the spokesman for Ifa around the world in his role as *Awishe Ogbaiye ,* states that "The word Takua is a corruption of the word Tapa, . . . a name for the Nupe people, who are immediately north-east of Yorubaland.

[13] This praise song was collected by the legendary ethnographer Lydia Cabrera in the 1950's in the highly regarded province of Matanzas, Cuba, known for keeping Yoruba retentions very zealously, See Cabrera, La Laguna Sagrada de San Joaquin(Madrid: Editorial "R", 1973), page 89

THE BOOK ON PALO

DEITIES, INITIATORY RITUALS AND CEREMONIES

BY RAUL CANIZARES

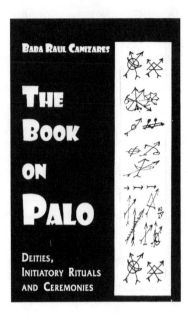

Palo Monte teaches trust in God, belief in destiny, and respect for the forces that move the Universe. The practice of Palo Monte engenders a particular form of spiritual strength, a gutsy, down-in-yourgroin, earthy power that some people need to experience as their souls travel on the way to the Final Cause. Those who have been blessed with a powerful Palo and Santeria foundation must lay aside the veil of secrecy that was used in the past in order to give the world a glimpse the beautiful traditions that comprise the religion. Our religion consists in belief in a high God whom we praise, a number of demigods who we actively worship and interact with, the pure spirits we constantly work with, a hierarchical priesthood, a body of believers, temples, altars, and traditional rituals passed on from generation to generation by way of our ancestors. We conduct ourselves according to a well-defined set of ethics and morals which teach respect for human life, the sharing of wealth with those who are less fortunate. Paleros believe that there is a clear and long-standing battle between absolute good and absolute evil, the tension between the two being the energy that propels existence. Pure spirits incarnate in the material world in order to live out their destiny here for as long as it is necessary in order to learn what can only be learned in the material plane, in order to advance to the realm of the spirits (also called the realm of the essences) or to the realm of Truth, from which no reincarnation is necessary. We maintain constant communication with enlightened essences in order to receive their guidance, wisdom, and beneficent care.

ISBN 0-942272-71-4 S"x 6" 160 pages $21.95

ORIGINAL PUBLICATIONS
TOLL FREE 1 (888) OCCULT-1 WWW.ORIGINALPUB.COM

POWERS OF THE ORISHAS

Santeria and the Worship of Saints

Migene GonzalezWippler

Item #005 - $8.95

Santeria is the Afro-Cuban religion based on an amalgamation between some of the magio-religious beliefs and practices of the Yoruba people and those of the Catholic church. In Cuba where the Yoruba proliferated extensively, they became known as *Lucumi,* a word that means "friendship".

Santeria is known in Cuba as Lucumi Religion. The original Yoruba language, interspersed with Spanish terms and corrupted through the centuries of misuse and mispronunciation, also became known as Lucumi. Today some of the terms used in Santeria would not be recognized as Yoruba in Southwestern Nigeria, the country of origin of the Yoruba people.

Santeria is a Spanish term that means a confluence of saints and their worship. These saints are in reality clever disguises for some of the Yoruba deities, known as Orishas. During the slave trade, the Yoruba who were brought to Cuba were forbidden the practice of their religion by their Spanish masters. In order to continue their magical and religious observances safely the slaves opted for the identification and disguise of the Orishas with some of the Catholic saints worshipped by the Spaniards. In this manner they were able to worship their deities under the very noses of the Spaniards without danger of punishment.

Throughout the centuries the practices of the Yoruba became very popular and soon many other people of the Americas began to practice the new religion.

ISBN 0-942272-25-0 5½"x 8½" 144 pages $8.95

ORIGINAL PUBLICATIONS

- ☐ HELPING YOURSELF WITH SELECTED PRAYERS *VOLUME 2*; $10.95
- ☐ THE BOOK ON PALO; Raul Canizares $21.95
- ☐ BRAZILIAN PALO PRIMER: Robert Laremy $6.95
- ☐ COMPLETE BOOK OF VOODOO; Robert Pelton $14.95
- ☐ THE CAULDRON OF DREAMS; Gerina Dunwich $6.95
- ☐ ORIGINAL PUBLICATIONS COMPLETE BATH BOOK - Canizares - $6.95
- ☐ THE PSALM WORKBOOK; Robert Laremy $7.95
- ☐ SPIRITUAL CLEANSINGS & PSYCHIC PROTECTION; Robert Laremy $7.95
- ☐ PAPA JIM'S HERBAL MAGIC WORKBOOK; Papa Jim $6.95
- ☐ LIFE & WORKS OF MARIE LAVEAU - Canizares $5.95
- ☐ RITUALS AND SPELLS OF SANTERIA; Wippler $8.95
- ☐ DREAM YOUR LUCKY LOTTERY NUMBER; Raul Canizares $5.95
- ☐ NEW REVISED MASTER BOOK OF CANDLEBURNING $5.95
- ☐ HELPING YOURSELF WITH SELECTED PRAYERS $6.95
- ☐ NEW REV. 6&7 BKS. OF MOSES; Wippler $9.95
- ☐ THE MAGIC CANDLE; Charmaine Dey $5.95
- ☐ VOODOO & HOODOO; by Jim Haskins - $12.95
- ☐ VOODOO CHARMS & TALISMANS; Robert Pelton $8.95
- ☐ MYSTERY OF LONG LOST 8, 9, 10 BOOKS OF MOSES - Gamache $5.95
- ☐ POWERFUL POTIONS OF SANTERIA; Carlos Montenegro -$7.95
- ☐ HELPING YOURSELF WITH MAGICAL OILS A-Z; Maria Solomon - $8.95
- ☐ INSTANT MONEY EMPOWERMENT; Maria Solomon - $6.95
- ☐ MONEY MAGIC; by Jade - $5.95
- ☐ LOVE CHARMS & SPELLS; by Jade - $5.95
- ☐ PROTECTION CHARMS & SPELLS; Jade $5.95
- ☐ POWERFUL PROTECTION MAGIC; Gary Brodsky - $6.95
- ☐ DREAM YOUR LUCKY LOTTERY NUMBER; Raul Canizares $5.95
- ☐ MAGICAL HERBAL BATHS OF SANTERIA; Montenegro $5.95
- ☐ SANTERIA; AFRICAN MAGIC IN LATIN AMERICA; Wippler $10.95
- ☐ SANTERIA EXPERIENCE; Wippler $8.95
- ☐ POWERS OF THE ORISHAS; Wippler $8.95
- ☐ SHANGO; Santeria and the Orisha of Thunder; Canizares $4.95
- ☐ ESHU- ELEGGUA; Santeria & Orisha of the Crossroads; Canizares $4.95
- ☐ OBATALA: Santeria & the White Robed King of Orisha; Canizares $4.95
- ☐ BABALU AYE; Santeria and the Lord of Pestilence; Canizares $4.95
- ☐ OSHUN: Santeria Orisha of Love, Rivers & Sensuality; Canizares $4.95
- ☐ OYA: Ifa and the Spirit of the Wind; Fatunmbi $4.95
- ☐ YEMAYA: Ifa and the Spirit of the Ocean; Fatunmbi $4.95

NAME _____ TELEPHONE _____

ADDRESS _____

CITY _____ STATE _____ ZIP _____

ORIGINAL PUBLICATIONS • P.O. BOX 236, OLD BETHPAGE, NY 11804-0236